THIS BOOK BELONGS TO

_____

_____

What do you actually want to say right now?

> # Are you seriously this incompetent?

Alternative

> Wow, you're really keeping things... interesting around here!

What do you actually want to say right now?

Who
put you
in charge?

Alternative

Leadership really
does come in a
ll forms, doesn't it?

What do you actually want to say right now?

If I have to explain this one more time, I'm going to lose it.

Alternative

Let's go over it again—third time's the charm, right?

What do you actually want to say right now?

I didn't call you stupid, I said that sounds like something a stupid person would say.

Alternative

I didn't mean you're stupid, just that your thought process is… avant-garde.

What do you actually want to say right now?

WTF part of 'I'm busy' didn't you understand?

Alternative

Which syllable of 'leave me alone' is giving you trouble?

What do you actually want to say right now?

> # Are you completely oblivious to what's happening?

Alternative

> I can see you're bringing a fresh perspective to this situation.

What do you actually want to say right now?

> # I'm not doing your job for you.

Alternative

> ## I'd be happy to support you once you've outlined your next steps.

What do you actually want to say right now?

> ## That's not how any of this works.

Alternative

> Hmm, an innovative approach! Let's explore if it aligns with our processes.

What do you actually want to say right now?

Do you
have a brain
cell left to rub together?

Alternative

You know what?
Let's brainstorm together—it might spark
something brilliant!

This is a disaster
waiting to happen.

Alternative

Well, this is shaping up
to be an exciting challenge!

What do you actually want to say right now?

Why are you still talking?

Alternative

Got it!
Let's pause here so
we can dive into action.

What do you actually want to say right now?

That's a you problem,
not a me problem.

Alternative

I trust you've
got this—let me know
how I can support from the
sidelines!

What do you actually want to say right now?

This makes zero sense.

Alternative

I think we're onto something—let's clarify the finer details a bit!

What do you actually want to say right now?

Wow, you really
dropped the ball
on that one.

Alternative

Looks like
we have a great opportunity
to recalibrate here!

What do you actually want to say right now?

> # Are you
> # even trying?

Alternative

> ## Let's strategize
> ## a bit more to
> ## really nail this down!

What do you actually want to say right now?

Can you
stop making
everything worse?

Alternative

Your enthusiasm
for hands-on experimentation
is truly unmatched!

What do you actually want to say right now?

> ## Seriously?
> ## That's what you're
> ## going with?

Alternative

> # Bold choice!
> # Let's workshop it
> # to perfection.

What do you actually want to say right now?

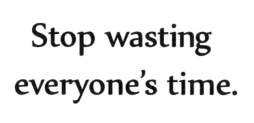

Stop wasting everyone's time.

Alternative

You're really committed to keeping the energy in this meeting alive!

Why do I have to fix your mistakes?

Alternative

Teamwork makes the dream work!
I'm just here to put on the finishing touches.

What do you actually want to say right now?

> # Please shut up already.

Alternative

> # Thanks for your input —let's get some other thoughts in the mix!

What do you actually want to say right now?

You clearly have
no idea what you're
talking about.

Alternative

You bring a unique lens to this
discussion—it's refreshing!

What do you actually want to say right now?

> # I can't believe
> # you still work here.

Alternative

> # Wow,
> # your dedication really
> # stands the test of time!

What do you actually want to say right now?

You're making
my job so much
harder.

Alternative

You're really
challenging me to level up
my multitasking skills!

What do you actually want to say right now?

That's a terrible plan.

Alternative

Hmm, it's ambitious! Let's refine it to make it actionable.

What do you actually want to say right now?

> # You don't know
> # what you're doing, do you?

Alternative

> # It looks like you're
> # figuring it out as you
> # go—we've all been there!

I'm not your babysitter.

Alternative

I see you're looking for guidance—happy to point you in the right direction.

What do you actually want to say right now?

How have you
managed to screw
this up again?

Alternative

Ah, a chance to iterate
and improve—what
a growth moment!

What do you actually want to say right now?

This is
the dumbest conversation
I've ever had.

Alternative

Well,
this is certainly an unconventional
approach to problem-solving!

What do you actually want to say right now?

Do you
even know what
the goal is?

Alternative

Let's revisit
the objectives to make sure
we're all on the same page!

What do you actually want to say right now?

Your incompetence
is exhausting.

Alternative

You've got a unique
way of keeping things... dynamic!

What do you actually want to say right now?

Why do you keep asking me
the same question?

Alternative

I think we covered this earlier,
but I'm happy to clarify one more time.

What do you actually want to say right now?

That's literally not how anything works.

Alternative

You're thinking outside the box— I admire the creativity!

What do you actually want to say right now?

You've officially
tested my last nerve.

Alternative

Wow,
you're really making me
dig deep into my patience toolkit!

What do you actually want to say right now?

How are you this clueless?

Alternative

Everyone has their strengths—let's figure out how to align yours here.

What do you actually want to say right now?

I'm about to
walk out.

Alternative

I think this is a great moment for a quick reset—back in five!

What do you actually want to say right now?

I can't deal with your nonsense today.

Alternative

Wow, you're really bringing the energy—
I'll need some coffee to keep up!

What do you actually want to say right now?

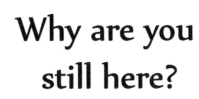

Why are you
still here?

Alternative

Your commitment to being present
is truly inspiring!

What do you actually want to say right now?

This project is a dumpster fire, and it's your fault.

Alternative

We're definitely in uncharted territory—let's turn this into a learning experience!

What do you actually want to say right now?

Stop pretending you know what you're doing.

Alternative

I love your confidence—let's back it up with some additional context.

What do you actually want to say right now?

You're the reason
I need therapy.

Alternative

Working with you has really
expanded my emotional resilience!

Do you actually do anything?

Alternative

Your behind-the-scenes contributions must be truly invaluable!

What do you actually want to say right now?

You've made everything worse, as usual.

Alternative

Your ability to keep things exciting is truly unmatched!

What do you actually want to say right now?

We don't have time for your BS today.

Alternative

Let's keep things focused—we've got a lot to tackle!

What do you actually want to say right now?

Are you seriously this bad at your job?

Alternative

Everyone's got room for growth—let's focus on next steps!

What do you actually want to say right now?

This makes me
want to scream into a pillow.

Alternative

I'm feeling passionately
inspired to find a solution right
now!

What do you actually want to say right now?

Why do you insist
on making everything harder?

Alternative

You really know how to challenge
my creative problem-solving skills!

Stop micromanaging me.

Alternative

I appreciate your attention to detail, but I've got this handled.

What do you actually want to say right now?

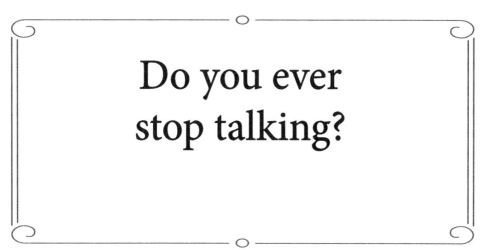

Do you ever stop talking?

Alternative

You're so thorough—I think we've got all we need for now!

I can't keep fixing your mess.

Alternative

Let's collaborate so we can streamline this process moving forward.

What do you actually want to say right now?

No one cares about your opinion.

Alternative

Interesting input! Let's see how it fits with the overall strategy.

What do you actually want to say right now?

This isn't rocket science!

Alternative

Let's break this down step by step to keep it simple.

What do you actually want to say right now?

You're the reason
deadlines exist.

Alternative

Your enthusiasm sometimes
gets ahead of the timeline—but we'll
catch up!

What do you actually want to say right now?

That's not
my problem.

Alternative

Let's figure out how
this fits into the bigger picture.

What do you actually want to say right now?

You really don't get it,
do you?

Alternative

I think there's an opportunity
here for some deeper understanding.

What do you actually want to say right now?

I need you to leave me alone right now.

Alternative

Let me wrap this up first, and then I'll be all yours!

What do you actually want to say right now?

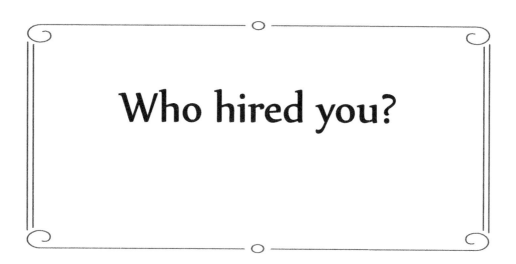

Who hired you?

Alternative

You bring such a... unique skill set to the table!

You're absolutely
terrible at this.

Alternative

Everyone has a learning curve—yours
just happens to be steeper than most!

What do you actually want to say right now?

Why do you keep overcomplicating everything?

Alternative

I admire your thoroughness, but let's try a more streamlined approach.

What do you actually want to say right now?

If I roll my eyes any harder,
they'll get stuck.

Alternative

I'm processing that idea—give me
a moment to absorb it fully!

What do you actually want to say right now?

> # That's not even close to being correct.

Alternative

> Hmm, I think we may need to refine this a bit—it's almost there!

What do you actually want to say right now?

I don't have time for your stupidity.

Alternative

Let's focus on the key priorities—I'm a little tight on time today!

What do you actually want to say right now?

You're a walking disaster.

Alternative

Your unpredictable approach always keeps things lively!

What do you actually want to say right now?

Your incompetence
is contagious.

Alternative

You've got such a unique
approach—it's almost inspiring!

What do you actually want to say right now?

This meeting
could have been an email.

Alternative

Great discussion!
Let's summarize this in a follow-up
email for clarity.

> If stupidity was a sport, you'd be a champion.

Alternative

> You've got a unique way of approaching challenges—truly one of a kind!

What do you actually want to say right now?

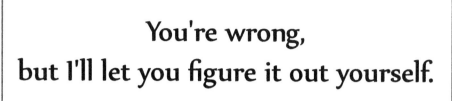

You're wrong,
but I'll let you figure it out yourself.

Alternative

Interesting!
Let's see how that approach works
out in real-time.

What do you actually want to say right now?

WTF are you even talking about?

Alternative

Wow, that's certainly... an idea! Could you elaborate a bit more?

What do you actually want to say right now?

Did you even read
my fcking email?

Alternative

Just circling back to the email
I sent earlier—happy to resend if needed!

What do you actually want to say right now?

You bring chaos wherever you go, but hey, at least you're consistent.

Alternative

You're like glitter—impossible to ignore and impossible to clean up.

What do you actually want to say right now?

I'd agree with you,
but then we'd both be wrong.

Alternative

I could agree with you,
but I don't like lying.

Printed in Great Britain
by Amazon

52660182R00040